# ROSA PARKS

KRISTEN SUSIENKA

**PowerKiDS**
press™

New York

Published in 2020 by The Rosen Publishing Group, Inc.
29 East 21st Street, New York, NY 10010

First Edition

Editor: Kristen Susienka
Book Design: Michael Flynn

Photo Credits: Cover, p. 1 William Philpott/Hulton Archive/Getty Images; series background Kharchenko Rusian/Shutterstock.com; pp. 5, 11, 17, 19 Bettmann/Getty Images; pp. 7, 9 The Washington Post/Getty Images; p. 13 (bus interior) Gino Santa Maria/Shutterstock.com; p. 13 (Claudette Colvin) https://en.wikipedia.org/wiki/Claudette_Colvin#/media/File:Claudette_Colvin.jpg; p. 15 UniversalImagesGroup/Getty Images; p. 21 PAUL SANCYA/AFP/Getty Images.

Library of Congress Cataloging-in-Publication Data

Names: Susienka, Kristen, author.
Title: Rosa Parks / Kristen Susienka.
Description: New York : PowerKids Press, 2020. | Series: African American
  leaders of courage | Includes index.
Identifiers: LCCN 2019013175| ISBN 9781725308541 (pbk.) | ISBN 9781725308565
  (library bound) | ISBN 9781725308558 (6 pack)
Subjects: LCSH: Parks, Rosa, 1913-2005–Juvenile literature. | African
  American women civil rights workers–Alabama–Montgomery–Biography–Juvenile literature. | African
  Americans–Alabama–Montgomery–Biography–Juvenile literature. | Civil rights workers–Alabama–Montgomery–
  Biography–Juvenile literature. | African Americans–Civil rights–Alabama–Montgomery–History–20th
  century–Juvenile literature. | Segregation in transportation–Alabama–Montgomery–History–20th century–Juvenile
  literature. | Montgomery (Ala.)–Race relations–Juvenile literature. | Montgomery (Ala.)–Biography–Juvenile literature.
Classification: LCC F334.M753 S87 2020 | DDC 323.092 [B] –dc23
LC record available at https://lccn.loc.gov/2019013175

Manufactured in the United States of America

CPSIA Compliance Information: Batch #CWPK20. For Further Information contact Rosen Publishing, New York, New York at 1-800-237-9932.

# CONTENTS

## A Brave Woman

Rosa Parks worked hard to end **segregation** in the 1950s and 1960s. She was part of the **civil rights movement**. She showed bravery by standing up for herself and others. She was a powerful role model.

5

## Life in Alabama

Rosa was born in 1913 and grew up in Alabama. She went to a segregated girls-only school. She wanted to be a teacher, but at 16, she had to leave school to care for her grandma and mom, who were sick.

childhood home of Rosa Parks

7

## Marriage and NAACP

In 1932, Rosa married Raymond Parks. He was working for **justice** for African Americans in Montgomery, Alabama. Rosa started doing so, too. She began working for Montgomery's **NAACP** group. People liked Rosa and thought she was strong.

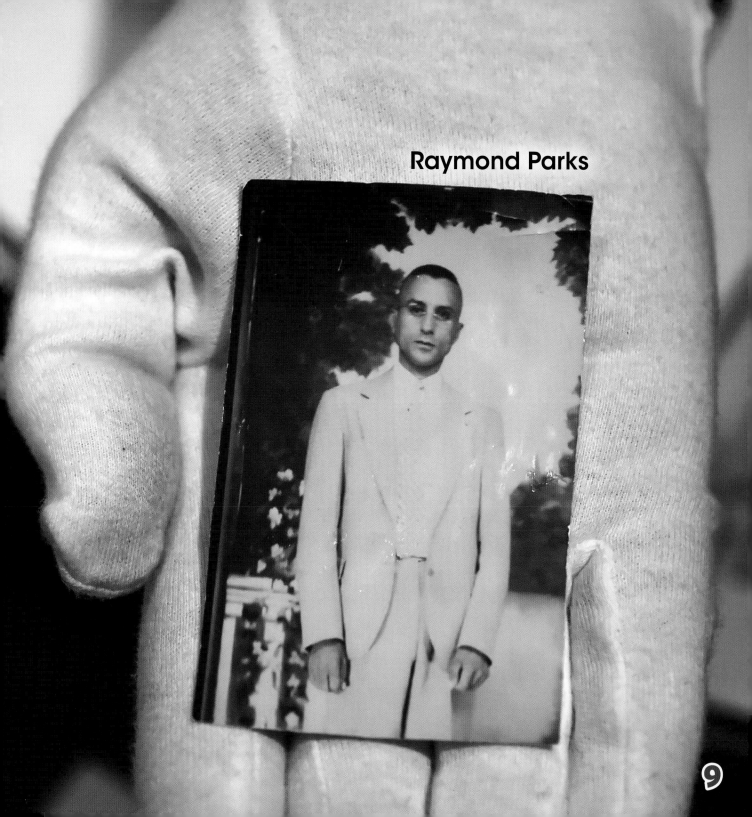

Raymond Parks

## Leading a Movement

Rosa became a leader in the civil rights movement. She helped African Americans in Montgomery work for justice. She met and worked with other leaders, such as Martin Luther King Jr. She also helped young people work for justice.

Martin Luther
King Jr.

11

# A Brave Act in March 1955

In March 1955, Claudette Colvin, a teenager whom Rosa knew, was sitting on a crowded Montgomery bus. A white woman got on the bus, and the driver told Claudette that she had to give up her seat. Claudette refused and was arrested.

Claudette Colvin

## December 1, 1955

Nine months later, Rosa did something much the same. A white man boarded the bus Rosa was riding and the driver told her to move. She refused. The driver called the police, and Rosa was arrested. Her story was shared around the world.

15

## Boycotting Buses

Within days, a **boycott** started in the city. Hundreds of African American men and women didn't ride the buses. They walked to work and school instead. The boycott lasted over a year. In 1956, the U.S. Supreme Court said segregation on buses was against the law.

# Truth Keeps Marching On

Rosa helped the civil rights movement even after her arrest. She marched and **protested** to end segregation everywhere. But it wasn't easy. She lost her job and dealt with bullies. In 1957, she and Raymond moved to Detroit, Michigan.

## A Strong Woman

Rosa worked for justice the rest of her life. She won many awards, including the Congressional Gold Medal. She also wrote an **autobiography**. She joined the National Women's Hall of Fame in 1993. She died in 2005, but people still remember her bravery today.

# THE LIFE OF ROSA PARKS

1913 — Rosa is born.

1932 — Rosa marries Raymond Parks.

1955 — Rosa refuses to give up her seat on a bus for a white man, setting off the Montgomery bus boycotts.

1993 — Rosa is welcomed into the National Women's Hall of Fame.

2005 — Rosa dies.

# GLOSSARY

**autobiography:** A book that tells the story of a person's life that is written by the person it is about.

**boycott:** A refusal to buy, use, or take part in something.

**civil rights movement:** A time period in U.S. history in which African Americans fought for equal civil rights, or the freedoms granted by law.

**NAACP:** National Association for the Advancement of Colored People, an organization that works for the civil rights of African Americans in the United States.

**justice:** Fair treatment.

**protest:** To stand up for a belief, usually publically.

**segregation:** The separation of people based on race, class, or ethnicity.

# INDEX

# WEBSITES

Due to the changing nature of Internet links, PowerKids Press has developed an online list of websites related to the subject of this book. This site is updated regularly. Please use this link to access the list: www.powerkidslinks.com/AALC/parks